CHINA ATLAS ROAD MAP 2024

Explore China And Its Neighborhood With The Details Road Map And Insider Planning Tips To Navigate The Country Like A Local

EDWARD RICK

Contents

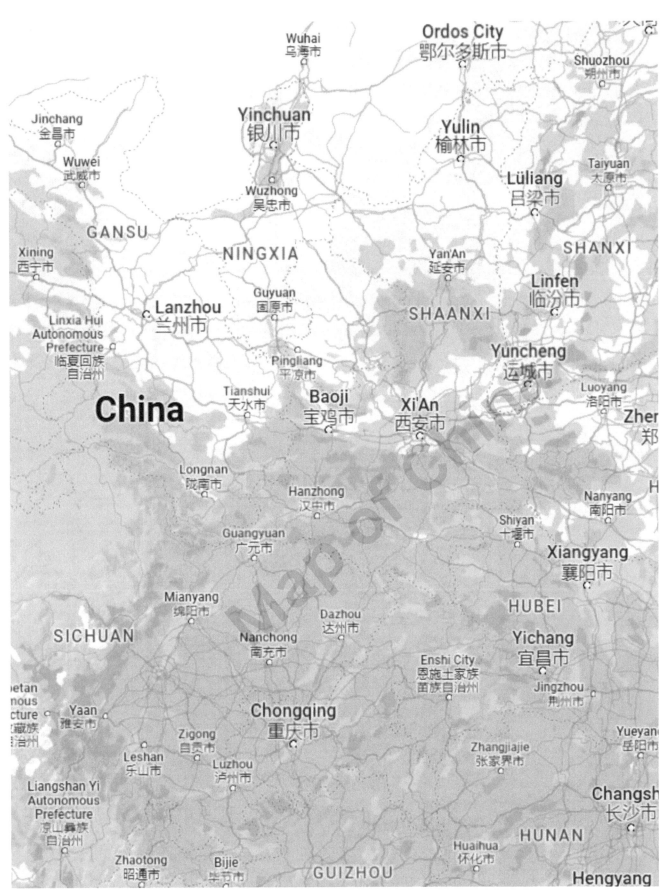

Beijing

Guangzhou

Chongqing

INTRODUCTION

Welcome to the "China Atlas Road Map 2024," a comprehensive guide that not only maps the vast and varied landscape of China but also marks a significant milestone in the evolution of cartography in this ancient land. This atlas is designed to be a friendly companion for both the curious traveler and the dedicated scholar, offering a window into the rich geographical tapestry that is China.

Overview of China's Geography and Significance of the 2024 Atlas

China's geography is as diverse as it is expansive. From the frozen tundras of the north to the tropical rainforests in the south, from the majestic Himalayas in the west to the bustling megacities in the east, China encompasses a world within its borders. The "China Atlas Road Map 2024" captures this diversity with detailed, up-to-date maps and information, reflecting the country's dynamic changes. This edition holds particular significance as it represents the latest advancements in Chinese cartography, providing an invaluable resource for navigation and understanding China's complex terrain.

The Evolution of Mapping in China

The art of mapping in China dates back over two millennia, with the earliest records indicating the use of maps for administration and military strategy. Over the centuries, Chinese cartographers have employed a variety of techniques and instruments to depict their world, from simple lodestones to sophisticated satellite imagery. The "China Atlas Road Map 2024" is based on the shoulders of these historical endeavors, embodying modern technology to offer precise and dependable cartographic data.

Objectives and Scope of this Guide

The primary objective of the "China Atlas Road Map 2024" is to give a detailed and attainable representation of China's geography. It aims to serve as a practical tool for navigation and planning, as well as a source of educational material for those looking to deepen their knowledge of China's geographical features. The scope of this atlas extends beyond mere topography; it delves into the cultural, historical, and economic aspects of the regions it covers, offering a holistic view of the nation.

Note: Maps are accessed by QR Code to Google map and it is easy to use

How To Use the Map With QR Code

❖ Scan the QR Code with your device

❖ A link will display on your device Click the link and it will direct you to the map

❖ On the screen interface Click on directions and enter your exact location at the starting point

❖ Select your means of transportation to your destination and follow the directions on the map

Tianjin

CHAPTER 1

Navigating China: The Basics

1. Visa Requirements

China requires most foreign travelers to obtain a visa before arrival. Here's what you need to know:

- ➤ Tourist Visa (L Visa): Apply at a Chinese embassy or consulate in your home country.
- ➤ Types of Visas: Single-entry or multiple-entry (choose based on your travel plans).
- ➤ Documents Needed: Passport, visa application form, recent photo, and travel itinerary.
- ➤ Duration: Usually 30 days, but extensions are possible.
- ➤ Tip: Apply well in advance to avoid last-minute stress.

2. Currency and Money Matters

Understanding China's currency and managing your finances:

- ➤ Currency: The official currency is the Chinese Yuan (CNY) or Renminbi (RMB).
- ➤ ATMs: Widely available in cities; check if your card works internationally.
- ➤ Cash vs. Cards: Carry some cash for small purchases; major cities accept credit cards.
- ➤ Exchange Rates: Exchange money at banks or authorized exchange counters.
- ➤ WeChat Pay and Alipay: Mobile payment apps are popular; set them up for convenience.

3. Local Customs and Etiquette

Respecting local culture and norms:

- ➤ Greetings: A simple nod or handshake suffices; avoid overly affectionate gestures.
- ➤ Chopsticks: Don't stick them upright in your food; it's considered bad luck.
- ➤ Shoes: Remove shoes when entering someone's home.
- ➤ Gifts: Present gifts with both hands; avoid clocks and white flowers.
- ➤ Queues: Be patient; cutting in line is frowned upon.

4. Language Basics

A few phrases go a long way:

> Hello: "Nǐ hǎo" (knee how)
> Thank You: "Xièxiè" (shieh-shieh)
> Yes: "Shì" (sher)
> No: "Bù shì" (boo sher)
> Numbers: Learn basic numbers for bargaining and ordering food.

5. Safety Tips

Stay safe during your travels:

> Traffic: Look both ways when crossing streets; traffic can be chaotic.
> Hygiene: Carry hand sanitizer and use it frequently.
> Scams: Be cautious of over-friendly strangers offering tours or deals.
> Food and Water: Stick to bottled water and eat at reputable places.
> Emergency Numbers: Know the local emergency hotline (110 for police, 120 for medical).

Packing List for China Travel: Seasons and Regions

1. Spring (March to May)

Essentials:

- Lightweight layers: T-shirts, long-sleeve shirts, and a light jacket.
- Comfortable walking shoes.
- Rain gear: Umbrella or waterproof jacket.
- Sunglasses and sunscreen.
- Optional:
- Scarf or shawl for chilly evenings.
- Hat for sun protection.
- Insect repellent for outdoor activities.

2. Summer (June to August)

Essentials:

- Lightweight, breathable clothing: Shorts, tank tops, and dresses.
- Sandals or comfortable sneakers.
- Sun hat and sunglasses.
- Swimsuit for beach destinations.

Optional:

- Portable fan or handheld fan.
- Reusable water bottle to stay hydrated.
- Lightweight rain jacket (for occasional summer showers).

3. Autumn (September to November)

Essentials:

- Layers: T-shirts, sweaters, and a medium-weight jacket.
- Comfortable walking shoes or boots.
- Scarf or pashmina for cooler evenings.
- Camera to capture fall foliage.
- Optional:
- Gloves and beanies for colder days.
- Power bank for charging devices on the go.

4. Winter (December to February)

Essentials:

- Warm clothing: Thermal layers, sweaters, and a heavy coat.
- Insulated boots or waterproof shoes.
- Hat, gloves, and scarf.
- Hand warmers for extremely cold days.

Optional:

- Portable phone charger (cold weather drains batteries faster).
- Hot packs for staying warm outdoors.

5. Regional Considerations

Beijing and Northern China:

✓ Pack for colder temperatures, especially in winter.
✓ Layers are essential due to temperature fluctuations.

Shanghai and Eastern China:

✓ Mild winters, but still pack warm clothing.
✓ Summers can be hot and humid.

Guilin and Southern China:

✓ Warm and humid year-round.
✓ Lightweight clothing and rain gear are crucial.

Tibet and Western China:

✓ High altitude and cold weather.
✓ Warm layers, sturdy boots, and sun protection.

Hiking Essentials

1. Footwear:

Hiking Boots or Trail Shoes: Sturdy footwear with good traction.

Extra Socks: Keep your feet dry during long hikes.

2. Clothing:

Moisture-Wicking Layers: T-shirts, lightweight long-sleeve shirts, and breathable pants.

Fleece or Insulated Jacket: For cooler altitudes.

Rain Jacket or Poncho: Be prepared for sudden showers.

Wide-Brim Hat or Cap: Sun protection.

3. Gear:

Daypack: Carry water, snacks, and essentials.

Hydration System or Water Bottle: Stay hydrated.

Sunscreen and Sunglasses: Protect against UV rays.

Trail Map or GPS Device: Know your route.

Visiting Temples

1. Modest Clothing:

Covered Shoulders and Knees: Respect temple etiquette.

Lightweight Scarf or Shawl: To cover up if needed.

Comfortable Shoes: You'll be walking and standing.

2. Accessories:

Hat or Sun Umbrella: Sun protection.

Small Bag or Pouch: Keep your belongings organized.

Camera or Smartphone: Capture the beautiful temples.

CHAPTER 2

The Land and Its People

Physical Geography: Mountains, Rivers, Deserts, and Plains

Mountains That Touch the Sky

China's mountains are not just natural wonders; they are the guardians of history, culture, and biodiversity. The Himalayas, which include the world's tallest peak, Mount Everest, form a natural border with Nepal and India. In the central west, the Kunlun Mountains stretch across the Tibetan Plateau, while the Tianshan Mountains rise in the northwest. Each range tells a story of geological marvels and human perseverance.

Rivers That Carve the Earth

The lifeblood of China's ecology and civilization, its rivers, flow like silken ribbons across the country. The Yangtze River, known locally as Changjiang, is the third-longest in the world, nourishing the land from the Tibetan Plateau to the East China Sea. The Yellow River, or Huanghe, meanders through the northern plains, witnessing the rise and fall of dynasties. These waterways are not just physical features; they are the cradle of Chinese culture.

Deserts That Whisper Tales of Time

China's deserts, such as the Gobi and the Taklamakan, are landscapes of solitude and survival. They remind us of the earth's raw beauty and the resilience of life. These vast expanses of sand and stone have been crossed by camel caravans and explorers, each grain of sand a testament to the passage of time.

Plains That Feed Nations

The plains of China are its agricultural heartland. The eastern plains and southern coasts are fertile grounds that have sustained generations. Here, the harmony between human toil and nature's bounty is evident in the patchwork of fields and the rhythm of seasons.

The People: A Tapestry of Cultures

China's geography is a canvas for the rich tapestry of its people. From the nomadic herders in the Mongolian steppes to the fishermen in the coastal provinces, each community adds a unique thread to the nation's cultural fabric. The land shapes their lives, and in turn, they shape the land.

Political Map - Provinces, Autonomous Regions, and Municipalities

The Provinces: Building Blocks of a Nation

China is divided into several provinces, each with its unique character and contribution to the nation's identity. These provinces are akin to states in other countries and play a crucial role in the governance and cultural life of China. From the coastal province of Fujian to the landlocked Yunnan, each province has its own governance, economy, and local customs that contribute to the rich mosaic of China.

Autonomous Regions: Celebrating Diversity

In addition to provinces, China recognizes five autonomous regions: Guangxi, Inner Mongolia, Ningxia, Xinjiang Uygur, and Tibet. These regions have a higher degree of legislative freedom and are home to significant populations of ethnic minorities. They are areas of incredible cultural richness and historical depth, offering a glimpse into the lives of ethnic groups that have called these lands home for centuries.

Municipalities: Urban Powerhouses

China's municipalities—Beijing, Chongqing, Shanghai, and Tianjin—are cities with provincial-level status. They are the dynamos of China's economic engine, centers of culture, and hubs of innovation. These cities are directly governed by the central government and are pivotal in China's global interactions.

Special Administrative Regions: Unique Entities

Lastly, the special administrative regions of Hong Kong and Macau maintain separate governing and economic systems from those of mainland China. These regions reflect the historical and contemporary influences that continue to shape them in unique ways.

Population Distribution and Demographic Trends

Population Distribution: Where People Roam

China's population is like a symphony, with millions of notes playing in harmony. But where do these notes resonate the most? Let's take a closer look:

Urban Centers: The cities hum with life. By the end of 2023, around 66% of the Chinese population resided in cities and towns—a dramatic increase from less than 20% in 1980. Imagine the bustling streets of Shanghai, the historic alleys of Beijing, and the neon glow of Shenzhen. These urban centers are magnets for dreams, opportunities, and connections.

Rural Areas: Beyond the city lights lie the quiet villages and fertile fields. Approximately 477 million people still live in rural areas, where traditions blend with the rhythm of nature. Here, farmers till the soil, families gather around communal tables, and ancient customs persist. Rural China is a tapestry of simplicity and resilience.

Demographic Trends: A Portrait of Change

Demography paints a vivid picture of a nation's past, present, and future. Let's explore the brushstrokes:

Aging Population: China's population pyramid is shifting. After the founding of the People's Republic of

China in 1949, the Chinese population grew rapidly. To manage this explosion, the controversial one-child policy was introduced in 1979. It effectively slowed population growth but also led to an older median age. Eventually, the policy was revised, and in 2015, it became a two-child policy. However, the birth rate remained volatile. By 2022, population growth dropped to -0.06%, influenced by factors like the coronavirus pandemic. The aging society will lead to a rising old-age dependency ratio, where two working adults will statistically support one person aged above 65 years by 2050.

Urbanization: Urbanization gained momentum after the reform and opening policy in 1978. By the end of 2023, around 933 million people lived in urban areas. The eastern and southeastern coastal regions led the way, but the western and central regions are catching up. The arc from Harbin to Guangdong houses the majority of China's population. Guangdong, with approximately 127 million people, takes the lead, followed by Shandong, Henan, and Jiangsu provinces.

province of Fujian

SCAN HERE

HOW TO USE QR CODE

- Open your phone's camera app or download scanner app from play store or apple store
- Point the camera at the QR code for a few seconds (no need to take a photo).
- A link should appear on the display, leading you to the location of the code

province of Yunnan

云南省财政厅
计算中心大楼

Dongxing Beiqiao Brg
东兴北桥

Kunming Maternal
and Child Center
昆明市妇幼保健院

云南省教育厅宿舍9幢

St

Buzhu Ln

Z

Rong Cheng Ji Tu
镕诚集团

Tieju Rd

Huashan S Rd
Wuhua Shanshang
五华山上

Zh

Shil

SCAN HERE

HOW TO USE QR CODE

- Open your phone's camera app or download scanner app from play store or apple store
- Point the camera at the QR code for a few seconds (no need to take a photo).
- A link should appear on the display, leading you to the location of the code

Guangxi China

SCAN HERE

HOW TO USE QR CODE

- Open your phone's camera app or download scanner app from play store or apple store
- Point the camera at the QR code for a few seconds (no need to take a photo).
- A link should appear on the display, leading you to the location of the code

Inner Mongolia China

Mongol Autonomous
ion Government K...
古自治区
〈停车场

People's Government
of Inner Mongolia
内蒙古自治区政府

Chilechuan Ave
动勒川大街

Chilechuan Ave

SCAN HERE

HOW TO USE QR CODE

- Open your phone's camera app or download scanner app from play store or apple store
- Point the camera at the QR code for a few seconds (no need to take a photo).
- A link should appear on the display, leading you to the location of the code

Ningxia China

SCAN HERE

HOW TO USE QR CODE

- Open your phone's camera app or download scanner app from play store or apple store
- Point the camera at the QR code for a few seconds (no need to take a photo).
- A link should appear on the display, leading you to the location of the code

Xinjiang China

a Union Building
~场联合大厦

Heping N Rd

ongshan Rd

Tianshan Rd

Xinjiang Airport (Group)
Company Ticket Office
新疆机场(集团)
公司售票处
Event ticket seller

Mingde Rd

Mingde Rd

e Rd

N Rd

SCAN HERE

HOW TO USE QR CODE

- Open your phone's camera app or download scanner app from play store or apple store
- Point the camera at the QR code for a few seconds (no need to take a photo).
- A link should appear on the display, leading you to the location of the code

Tibet China

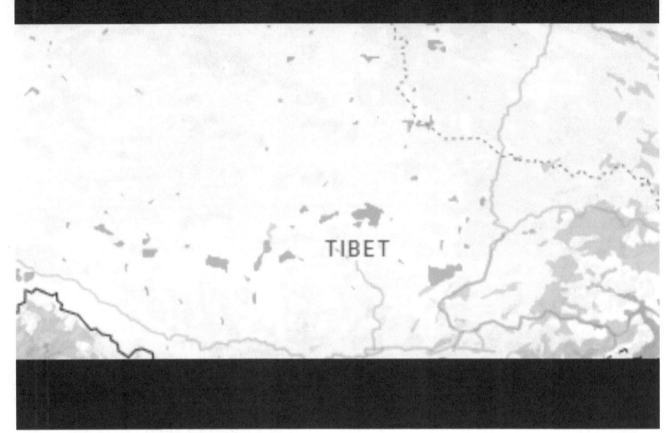

TIBET

SCAN HERE

HOW TO USE QR CODE

- Open your phone's camera app or download scanner app from play store or apple store
- Point the camera at the QR code for a few seconds (no need to take a photo).
- A link should appear on the display, leading you to the location of the code

Himalayas mountain

Himalayas Mountain

Himalayas
Famous range
with Mount
Everest

SCAN HERE

HOW TO USE QR CODE

- Open your phone's camera app or download scanner app from play store or apple store
- Point the camera at the QR code for a few seconds (no need to take a photo).
- A link should appear on the display, leading you to the location of the code

CHAPTER 3

The Silk Road Revival

Historical Significance of the Silk Road

The Ancient Silk Road: A Pathway of Prosperity

The Silk Road was not a single route but a vast network of trade paths that connected the East and West, stretching from the heart of China to the Mediterranean Sea. Established during the Han Dynasty around 130 B.C., it was a conduit for goods, ideas, and cultures for over a millennium.

Silk, the namesake of this road, was just one of the many treasures that traveled these routes. Gold, silver, wool, and precious stones made their way to China, while silk, tea, and porcelain journeyed to the far reaches of Rome and beyond. But the Silk Road carried more than just merchandise; it was a bridge for knowledge, art, religion, and technology, shaping civilizations along its length.

The Silk Road's Impact on History

The Silk Road's influence on history is profound. It facilitated the spread of Buddhism from India to China and saw the flow of scientific knowledge and artistic traditions across continents. Towns along the route, like Samarkand and Dunhuang, blossomed into hubs of multicultural exchange, where ideas and innovations were as traded as goods.

Revival in the Modern Era

Today, the spirit of the Silk Road is being revived with initiatives like the Belt and Road Initiative (BRI), aiming to enhance regional connectivity and embrace the cultural and economic ties that once flourished. This modern revival seeks to create a new era of trade and cultural exchange, echoing the historical significance of the ancient routes

The Belt and Road Initiative - Routes and Countries Involved

The Silk Road Economic Belt and the 21st Century Maritime Silk Road

The BRI is a global development strategy adopted by the Chinese government, involving infrastructure development and investments in countries in Europe,

Asia, Africa, the Middle East, and the Americas. The initiative has two main components: the land-based "Silk Road Economic Belt" and the sea-based "21st Century Maritime Silk Road."

The Silk Road Economic Belt connects China with Central Asia, Russia, and Europe. It passes through the mountainous regions of Central Asia and reaches as far as the Baltic Sea, the Mediterranean Sea, and the Arctic Ocean.

The 21st Century Maritime Silk Road is designed to go from China's seacoast to Europe through the South China Sea and the Indian Ocean in one route, and from China's seacoast through the South China Sea to the South Pacific in the other.

Countries Involved in the BRI

As of 2020, 138 countries have joined the BRI by signing a Memorandum of Understanding (MoU) with China. These countries span across all continents:

- Sub-Saharan Africa: 38 countries
- Europe & Central Asia: 34 countries, including 18 from the European Union

- East Asia & Pacific: 25 countries
- Middle East & North Africa: 17 countries
- Latin America & Caribbean: 18 countries
- South East Asia: 6 countries

Major Projects Under the BRI

Several significant projects have been developed under the BRI, including:

China-Pakistan Economic Corridor (CPEC): A collection of infrastructure projects that are currently under construction throughout Pakistan.

China–Mongolia–Russia Economic Corridor: A trilateral agreement to build an economic corridor between the three countries.

New Eurasia Land Bridge: An international passageway that links the Pacific and the Atlantic, running from Eastern China to Rotterdam in the Netherlands.

The Global Reach of the BRI

The BRI is truly a global endeavor, with the Democratic Republic of the Congo being the most recent country to join the initiative. The reach of the BRI is not limited to the countries that have signed MoUs; it also impacts the global economy and geopolitics, influencing trade routes, investment flows, and diplomatic relations.

Economic, Political, and Cultural Impacts of the Belt and Road Initiative

Economic Impact

The BRI is not merely a collection of infrastructure projects; it's an economic lifeline that spans continents. Here's how it has left its mark:

Infrastructure Investment: The BRI has supported the construction of airports, ports, power plants, bridges, railways, roads, and telecommunications networks across Eurasia, Latin America, and Africa. These projects enhance connectivity, facilitate trade, and boost economic growth in participating countries.

Job Creation: While Chinese contractors and construction companies often lead these projects, the BRI has created more than 400,000 jobs in host countries. These employment opportunities have helped lift over 40 million people out of poverty, fostering economic development and stability.

Political Influence

The BRI is not just about concrete and steel; it's a geopolitical chessboard where moves have global implications:

China's Sphere of Influence: While China emphasizes economic collaboration, many in the West view the BRI as a strategy to expand China's sphere of economic and political influence. By connecting regions across land and sea, China strengthens its ties with participating countries, shaping diplomatic relations and alliances.

U.S.-China Rivalry: The BRI is a tool in the broader U.S.-China rivalry. Geopolitical tensions underpin its execution, especially in the global South. The United States closely monitors China's outreach, wary of any reduction in Western influence among developing nations. Navigating this delicate balance is crucial for China to maintain relationships in the global arena.

Cultural Exchange

Beyond infrastructure and politics, the BRI fosters cultural exchange and understanding:

Soft Connectivity: The BRI extends beyond physical infrastructure. It encompasses rules, standards, and people-to-people exchanges. China strategically uses soft power to build bridges of understanding. However, suspicions persist, especially from the United States, which views China's outreach as geopolitical maneuvering.

Enhancing Soft Connectivity: High-quality BRI construction requires enhancing the soft connectivity of rules. By aligning standards, legal systems, and cultural exchange, the BRI promotes harmonious cooperation. China's role as both a developmental aid provider and a geopolitical player adds complexity to this delicate dance.

CHAPTER 4

Urbanization and Megacities

Growth of Megacities: Beijing, Shanghai, and Guangzhou

This section explores the pulsating heart of China's urbanization and the rise of its megacities. Beijing, Shanghai, and Guangzhou are not just cities; they are colossal hubs of humanity, each with a story that echoes China's journey from ancient civilization to modern superpower.

Beijing: The Imperial Metropolis

Beijing, the capital city, is a blend of the ancient and the futuristic. With a history that spans over three millennia, Beijing has transformed from the seat of emperors to a modern metropolis while preserving its cultural heritage. The city's urbanization has been a careful dance between maintaining its historical sites like the Forbidden City and embracing modernity with structures like the Bird's Nest Stadium. Despite recent trends showing a slight contraction in permanent residents, Beijing remains a political and cultural powerhouse, influencing trends and policies across China and beyond.

Shanghai: The Dragon's Head

Shanghai, known as the "Dragon's Head," is the epitome of China's economic might. It is a city that never sleeps, with skyscrapers that pierce the clouds and streets that buzz with commerce. As China's financial hub, Shanghai has seen explosive growth, particularly in its GDP, reflecting the meteoric ascent of the Chinese economy. The city's population has grown alongside its economy, although it too has experienced a recent dip in permanent residents. Nevertheless, Shanghai continues to be a magnet for businesses and individuals seeking opportunities in a city that symbolizes China's global aspirations.

Guangzhou: The Southern Gateway

Guangzhou, the southern gateway to China, is a city of trade and tradition. It has been a commercial center for centuries, dating back to the Maritime Silk Road. Today, Guangzhou is a megacity that thrives on innovation and international trade. Its urbanization has been marked by the growth of industries and the expansion of its metropolitan area. Guangzhou's population has surged, making it one of the most populous cities in China, although it too has seen a recent trend of negative growth in permanent residents. Despite this, Guangzhou remains a vital link in China's connection to the world, with its ports bustling with global commerce.

The Urban Symphony

The growth of Beijing, Shanghai, and Guangzhou into megacities is a testament to China's urbanization. These cities are more than just dots on a map; they are dynamic entities that pulse with the lives of millions. They are centers of power, commerce, and culture that have risen to meet the challenges of the 21st century

Urban Planning and Infrastructure Development

Urban planning in China is a grand vision turned into reality. It is the blueprint that shapes the growth of cities, balancing the needs of development with the preservation of history and the environment. The planning process is meticulous, involving experts from various fields to ensure that the expansion of cities is sustainable, efficient, and harmonious with the cultural ethos of the region.

Sustainable Urban Environments: China's urban planning prioritizes sustainability. Green spaces, public parks, and eco-friendly buildings are integral to new developments. The aim is to create urban environments that promote well-being and reduce the ecological footprint.

Integrated Transportation Networks: The development of integrated transportation networks is a cornerstone of China's urban planning. High-speed rail, subways, and bus systems are designed to connect people and places swiftly and comfortably, reducing traffic congestion and pollution.

Cultural Preservation: Amidst modernization, China's urban planning also focuses on preserving cultural heritage. Ancient landmarks, historical districts, and traditional architecture are protected and integrated into the urban landscape, maintaining the soul of the city.

The Backbone of Growth: Infrastructure Development

Infrastructure development in China is nothing short of revolutionary. It is the backbone that supports China's rapid urbanization and economic growth.

Investment in Public Infrastructure: China has invested heavily in public infrastructure, with an investment of seven trillion Yuan ($1.03 trillion) during its 12th Five-Year Plan from 2011 to 2015. This investment has fueled the construction of roads, bridges, airports, and other critical infrastructure.

Impact on Urbanization: The provision of infrastructure has had a profound impact on urbanization rates and land prices in China. Both intra-city and inter-city developments, such as express highways and railways, have spurred urban expansion and increased accessibility.

Challenges and Future Directions: Despite the progress, challenges remain. The quality of urban infrastructure needs improvement, and there is a push towards diversifying ownership and financing models to ensure sustainable development. Public-private partnerships and market finance are being explored to address these challenges.

Challenges and Opportunities of Rapid Urbanization

Rapid urbanization in China has brought about several challenges that require careful management and innovative solutions:

The strain on Infrastructure: The swift influx of people into urban areas has put a significant strain on existing infrastructure. Cities are grappling with the need for more housing, expanded transportation networks, and increased energy and water supplies.

Environmental Concerns: The environmental impact of urbanization is profound. Air and water pollution, waste management, and the loss of green spaces are pressing issues that cities must address to ensure sustainable development.

Social Services: Providing adequate health care, education, and social services to the growing urban population, including migrants, is a monumental task that strains municipal finances and resources.

Economic Disparities: While urbanization has lifted many out of poverty, it has also exacerbated income inequalities. The gap between the rich and poor, and between urban and rural residents, poses a challenge to social cohesion.

Opportunities Amidst Urban Expansion

Despite these challenges, rapid urbanization also presents numerous opportunities for China:

Economic Growth: Urban centers are powerhouses of economic activity, contributing significantly to GDP. They are hubs of innovation, commerce, and industry, driving national growth.

Demographic Dividends: Cities tend to have a younger and more economically active population. This demographic advantage can be harnessed to capture economic dividends and spur further development.

Cultural Exchange: Urbanization brings together people from diverse backgrounds, fostering a melting pot of cultures, ideas, and creativity.

Improved Quality of Life: For many, moving to cities means access to better jobs, education, and health care, leading to an improved quality of life and new opportunities.

Navigating the Urban Future

China's approach to managing urbanization involves balancing the challenges with the opportunities. Strategies such as sustainable urban planning, investment in public infrastructure, and policies aimed at equitable growth are critical. The nation's ability to navigate the complexities of urbanization will significantly influence its future trajectory.

Beijing China

Zhengyi Rd

Beijing E Jiaomin
Ln Restaurant Office...
北京东交民巷
饭店写字楼

a The Supreme
People's Court
最高人民法院

SCAN HERE

HOW TO USE QR CODE

- Open your phone's camera app or download scanner app from play store or apple store
- Point the camera at the QR code for a few seconds (no need to take a photo).
- A link should appear on the display, leading you to the location of the code

Shanghai China

SCAN HERE

HOW TO USE QR CODE

- Open your phone's camera app or download scanner app from play store or apple store
- Point the camera at the QR code for a few seconds (no need to take a photo).
- A link should appear on the display, leading you to the location of the code

Guangzhou China

SCAN HERE

HOW TO USE QR CODE

- Open your phone's camera app or download scanner app from play store or apple store
- Point the camera at the QR code for a few seconds (no need to take a photo).
- A link should appear on the display, leading you to the location of the code

CHAPTER 5

The Great Wall and Beyond

The Great Wall: History, Length, and Significance

The Great Wall of China, a series of fortifications made of stone, brick, tamped earth, wood, and other materials, is a marvel of military architecture and human endeavor. It stretches over rugged mountains and winds across deserts, extending approximately 13,000 miles from east to west in China.

The Origins: A Defensive Bulwark

The history of the Great Wall is rooted in the Warring States Period (475-221 BC) when several states built fortified walls to protect their territories. When Emperor Qin Shi Huang unified China in 221 BC, he ordered the removal of the walls that divided his empire and linked the remaining fortifications along the northern border to fend off invasions. This marked the beginning of the Great Wall as a national project.

The Construction: A Herculean Task

The construction of the Great Wall was a colossal undertaking. It involved millions of workers, including soldiers, peasants, and prisoners. The wall was built using local resources, and its design varied according to the terrain. In some areas, it featured double walls for extra security and included watchtowers and barracks for troops.

The Ming Dynasty: The Wall's Zenith

The most well-known sections of the Great Wall were built during the Ming Dynasty (1368-1644 AD). To protect against Mongol incursions, the Ming emperors fortified the wall with stronger materials and constructed a more sophisticated defense system, including cannons.

The Significance: Beyond Defense

While the Great Wall never fully prevented invasions, it became a symbol of the Chinese civilization's resilience and engineering prowess. It represented the boundary between the agricultural Chinese and the nomadic tribes to the north. Today, it stands as a testament to China's historical strength and is a UNESCO World Heritage site, attracting millions of visitors each year.

The Legacy: A Cultural Phenomenon

The Great Wall transcends its original military purpose. It has inspired countless works of art, literature, and folklore. It embodies the spirit of the Chinese people and their continuous pursuit of unity and protection of their cultural heritage.

Other Historical Landmarks and UNESCO World Heritage Sites

A Legacy Carved in Stone and Earth

China's historical landmarks are not just places; they are stories set in stone, earth, and time. They are the silent witnesses to China's enduring history and cultural evolution.

The Forbidden City: A Palace of Power

In the heart of Beijing lies the Forbidden City, a palatial complex that served as the imperial palace for the Ming and Qing dynasties. With its 980 surviving buildings and 8,704 rooms, it is a testament to the architectural genius and the hierarchical society of imperial China.

The Terracotta Army: Warriors for Eternity

The Mausoleum of the First Qin Emperor is home to the Terracotta Army, a collection of terracotta sculptures depicting the armies of Qin Shi Huang, the first Emperor of China. This site reveals the emperor's power and the artistic craftsmanship of ancient China.

The Potala Palace: A Sacred Sanctuary

Perched on Marpo Ri hill in Lhasa, the Potala Palace is a symbol of Tibetan Buddhism and the traditional residence of the Dalai Lama. Its towering white and red walls house thousands of rooms filled with art and scriptures, embodying the spiritual devotion of the Tibetan people.

The Summer Palace: An Imperial Garden

The Summer Palace in Beijing is an imperial garden known for its harmonious blend of natural landscape and artificial features. It is a masterpiece of Chinese garden design and has been a retreat for emperors seeking solace and inspiration.

The Temple of Heaven: A Celestial Altar

The Temple of Heaven in Beijing is where emperors performed heavenly rituals. It is an architectural wonder and a symbol of the relationship between heaven and earth, as perceived by the ancient Chinese.

Natural Wonders: A Canvas of Biodiversity

China's natural heritage sites are as diverse as its cultural landmarks:

Mount Huangshan: Known for its peculiarly shaped granite peaks, Mount Huangshan is celebrated for its scenic beauty and its role in Chinese art and literature.

Jiuzhaigou Valley: A fairy-tale landscape of multi-level waterfalls, colorful lakes, and snow-capped peaks, Jiuzhaigou Valley is a haven of biodiversity and natural wonders.

Sichuan Giant Panda Sanctuaries: These sanctuaries are the most important sites for the conservation of the giant panda, one of the world's most beloved endangered species.

The Cultural Landscape: A Harmony of Human and Nature

Honghe Hani Rice Terraces: These terraces in Yunnan Province are a reflection of profound knowledge of the environment and an adaptive agricultural practice that has persisted for over a millennium.

Fujian Tulou: These are large, enclosed, and fortified earth buildings, housing entire communities. They represent a unique communal living and defensive structure.

Preservation Efforts and Tourism

Safeguarding the Past for the Future

China's preservation efforts are a testament to its commitment to safeguarding its historical legacy for future generations. These efforts enclose a range of activities:

Restoration Projects: Restoration of ancient structures and landmarks is carried out with meticulous care, often using traditional materials and techniques to maintain authenticity.

Legislation for Protection: China has enacted laws and regulations to protect its cultural heritage. These laws ensure that any development or tourism activities do not compromise the integrity of historical sites.

International Collaboration: China works with international organizations like UNESCO to preserve its World Heritage Sites, ensuring that these treasures of human history remain intact.

Tourism: A Gateway to Cultural Discovery

Tourism in China is not just an economic activity; it's a gateway to cultural discovery and understanding:

Economic Engine: Tourism is a significant contributor to China's economy, providing jobs and spurring development in regions rich in cultural heritage.

Cultural Ambassador: Through tourism, China showcases its history and culture to the world, fostering global appreciation and understanding of its traditions.

Educational Platform: Tourists visiting historical sites learn about China's past, the significance of preservation, and the importance of cultural diversity.

Balancing Act: Conservation and Development

The challenge lies in balancing conservation efforts with the development of tourism:

Managing Visitor Impact: High tourist footfall can lead to wear and tear on historical sites. China employs strategies like visitor caps and off-season promotions to manage the impact.

Sustainable Tourism: China is increasingly adopting sustainable tourism practices, ensuring that tourism development does not come at the cost of environmental degradation or cultural dilution.

Community Involvement: Local communities are involved in preservation and tourism, providing them with a stake in the conservation of their heritage and benefiting economically from tourism.

The Ming Dynasty

Forbidden City Palace

Forbidden City Palace, China

View larger map

Ming & Qing dynasty palace with a museum

The Palace Museum
故宫博物院

Hall of Literary Brilliance
文华殿

Zhendumen
贞度门  太和门 昭德门

f Martial Valor
武英殿

Hall of Literary Brilliance
文华殿

n'anmen

SCAN HERE

HOW TO USE QR CODE

- **Open your phone's camera app or download scanner app from play store or apple store**
- **Point the camera at the QR code for a few seconds (no need to take a photo).**
- **A link should appear on the display, leading you to the location of the code**

The Potala Palace

The Potala Palace, China

View larger map

Potala Palace
布达拉宫

Sheng Di Kang
Sang Shop
圣地康桑商店
Clothing store

The Potala
Palace
布达拉宫

Potala Palace
Treasures Museum
布达拉宫珍宝馆

Nire Cold Noodles With

SCAN HERE

HOW TO USE QR CODE

- Open your phone's camera app or download scanner app from play store or apple store
- Point the camera at the QR code for a few seconds (no need to take a photo).
- A link should appear on the display, leading you to the location of the code

Summer Palace

Summer Palace, China

SCAN HERE

HOW TO USE QR CODE

- Open your phone's camera app or download scanner app from play store or apple store
- Point the camera at the QR code for a few seconds (no need to take a photo).
- A link should appear on the display, leading you to the location of the code

The Temple of Heaven

Temple of Heaven, China

View larger map

Temple of Heaven 天坛公园

天坛餐厅 Chinese

Zhaigong Ticket Office 斋宫售票处

SCAN HERE

HOW TO USE QR CODE

- Open your phone's camera app or download scanner app from play store or apple store
- Point the camera at the QR code for a few seconds (no need to take a photo).
- A link should appear on the display, leading you to the location of the code

Emperor Qinshihuang's Mausoleum Site Museum

Emperor Qinshihuang's Mausoleum Site Museum

View larger map

Emperor Qinshihuang's
Mausoleum Site Museum
秦始皇帝陵博物院

Terra-Cotta
Warriors
Museum
秦始皇兵马俑
博物馆

Youyi Sho
友谊商店

SCAN HERE

HOW TO USE QR CODE

- **Open your phone's camera app or download scanner app from play store or apple store**
- **Point the camera at the QR code for a few seconds (no need to take a photo).**
- **A link should appear on the display, leading you to the location of the code**

CHAPTER 6

Transportation Networks

Overview of China's Transportation Infrastructure

This part navigates the intricate web of China's transportation infrastructure, a cornerstone of its rapid development and modernization.

The Arteries of Growth: Roads and Highways

China's road network is the backbone of its transportation system. As of 2022, the length of China's highways exceeded 177,000 kilometers, making it one of the most extensive in the world. These roads connect the bustling cities, remote villages, and everything in between, facilitating the movement of goods and people across the country.

The Lifeline: Railways

China's railways are a lifeline that pulses with the rhythm of progress. The country has made significant strides in developing high-speed rail, with over 45,000 kilometers of high-speed railways as of 2022. These trains glide across the landscape at speeds up to 350 km/h, shrinking distances and knitting together the vast nation.

The Gateway: Airports

Air transport infrastructure has soared to new heights, with 254 civil airports in operation as of 2022. These airports serve as gateways to China and the world, with five airports handling more than 20 million passengers annually. They are the hubs from which China reaches out to the skies.

The Veins: Waterways

China's water transport infrastructure is robust, with the Yangtze River being the main artery for inland water transport. The country boasts approximately 64,800 kilometers of inland waterways, with the Yangtze River Delta serving as the largest and busiest port cluster globally.

The Shift: Towards Green Transportation

As China's transportation infrastructure expands, the focus is shifting towards sustainability. The government is investing in green transportation systems, as outlined in its 14th Five-Year Plan (2021-25). This includes high-speed rail, electric vehicle charging stations, and even China's first bicycle highway in Beijing.

The Impact: On the Economy and Society

The development of transportation infrastructure has had a profound impact on China's economy and society. It has facilitated economic growth, regional development, and urbanization. The transportation network has also influenced the social fabric, bringing people closer and fostering cultural exchange.

The Challenge: Balancing Development and Environment

As China's transportation network grows, balancing development with environmental conservation becomes crucial. The expansion has led to concerns over pollution and greenhouse gas emissions, prompting the government to take measures to create a smart and green transportation system.

Detailed Maps of Highways, Railways, and Air Routes

Highways: The Vast Network

China's highway system is a marvel of modern engineering, connecting remote areas with urban centers. The detailed maps in this atlas showcase the extensive network of national expressways, like the G101 from Beijing to Shenyang, and the G201 from Shanghai to Chengdu. These highways are the lifeblood of domestic trade and travel, facilitating the swift movement of goods and people across the country.

Railways: The Iron Veins

The railway maps in this atlas highlight the impressive expanse of China's rail system. High-speed rail lines, such as the Beijing-Shanghai route, are prominently featured, illustrating the speed and efficiency with which one can traverse the country. The maps also detail the vast network of conventional rail lines that reach into the less accessible regions, ensuring connectivity and development opportunities for all.

Air Routes: The Sky's Pathways

The air route maps provide a bird's-eye view of China's air traffic. Major hubs like Beijing Capital International Airport, Shanghai Pudong International Airport, and Guangzhou Baiyun International Airport serve as the primary nodes in this aerial network. The maps detail the domestic and international routes that emanate from these centers, connecting China to the world.

A Symphony of Movement

Together, these maps compose a symphony of movement, a testament to China's commitment to connectivity and progress. They are not just representations of physical routes but symbols of the nation's journey towards an integrated and accessible future.

As you peruse the detailed maps in the "China Atlas Road Map 2024," let them guide you through the landscapes of China's transportation networks. They are the arteries, veins, and pathways that pulse with the life of a nation on the move, a nation that continues to build bridges, lay tracks, and chart new courses in the sky.

Navigating the Future

The detailed maps serve as more than just navigational tools; they are a window into the future. They show us where China has been and where it is going, charting a course of development that is both ambitious and forward-thinking. As we turn the pages of this atlas, we are not just following roads, rails, and air routes; we are following the trajectory of a nation poised for continued growth and innovation.

Future Projects and International Connectivity

China's vision for the future of transportation is ambitious and forward-looking. The country's 14th Five-Year Plan outlines a roadmap for building and strengthening roads, railways, ports, and waterways, along with the technology and human capital that support the industry. Here are some key future projects:

High-Speed Rail Expansion: China plans to add 2,500 km of new high-speed railways in 2023 alone, with projects like the Sichuan-Xizhang Railway set to accelerate development in the southwest.

Comprehensive Transportation Network: By 2035, China aims to have a total of 700,000 kilometers of transportation networks, including railways, roads, airports, and commute hubs.

Intelligent Transportation: The focus is also on developing intelligent transportation technology and low-carbon transportation options to create a more sustainable future.

Connecting with the World: International Connectivity

China's international connectivity is a critical aspect of its transportation infrastructure, facilitating global trade and cultural exchange:

Belt and Road Initiative: This initiative continues to be a cornerstone of China's international connectivity, with ongoing projects to improve land bridges and connectivity between major urban areas and inland provinces.

Global 1-2-3 Logistics Circle: This program aims to bolster China's role in global trade by developing a modern, high-quality, and comprehensive national transport network.

International Transport Hubs: Plans are underway to construct about 20 international comprehensive transport hub cities, which will serve as key nodes in the global transportation network.

The Horizon of Opportunities

The future projects and international connectivity efforts are not just about creating a network of routes; they are about opening horizons of opportunities. They represent China's commitment to playing a leading role in global transportation, fostering economic growth, and promoting sustainable development.

China Highway

View larger map

Shehe S R...

Season Ba

China Highway
中国公路

Yudai Rd

路

Aomen Rd

Generou
丰

SCAN HERE

HOW TO USE QR CODE

- **Open your phone's camera app or download scanner app from play store or apple store**
- **Point the camera at the QR code for a few seconds (no need to take a photo).**
- **A link should appear on the display, leading you to the location of the code**

China Railways

View larger map

China Railway (High
Speed Train Station)

SCAN HERE

HOW TO USE QR CODE

- Open your phone's camera app or download scanner app from play store or apple store
- Point the camera at the QR code for a few seconds (no need to take a photo).
- A link should appear on the display, leading you to the location of the code

China Airlines

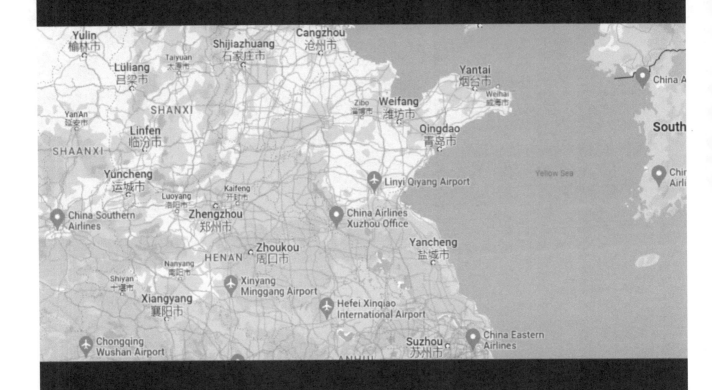

SCAN HERE

HOW TO USE QR CODE

- Open your phone's camera app or download scanner app from play store or apple store
- Point the camera at the QR code for a few seconds (no need to take a photo).
- A link should appear on the display, leading you to the location of the code

CHAPTER 7

Economic Powerhouses

China's Economic Zones and Industrial Hubs

This section delves into the engines that drive China's economic might—its special economic zones (SEZs) and industrial hubs.

The SEZs: Catalysts for Economic Reform

China's SEZs are regions with economic policies that are more free-market-oriented than the rest of the country. These zones were established to attract foreign investment and technology, and they have been pivotal in China's economic transformation. The first SEZs, such as Shenzhen, Xiamen, and Hainan, were established in the early 1980s and have since become models of rapid economic growth.

Contributions to the Economy

The SEZs have made significant contributions to China's GDP, employment, exports, and foreign direct investment (FDI). It is evaluated that as of 2007, SEZs accounted for about 22% of national GDP, 46% of FDI, and 60% of exports, generating over 30 million jobs. They have also played a crucial role in prompting new technologies in China and adopting modern management practices.

Industrial Clusters: Competitive Engines

Industrial clusters are geographic concentrations of interconnected companies, specialized suppliers, service providers, and associated institutions in a particular field. China's industrial clusters have been competitive engines for the local economy, fostering innovation, and driving the development of small and medium-sized enterprises.

High-Tech Development Zones

China has established numerous High-Tech Development Zones (HIDZs), which host a significant number of high-tech firms and science and technology incubators. These zones are vital for China's innovation strategy and contribute substantially to the high-tech industrial output and exports.

Economic and Technological Development Zones

The Economic and Technological Development Zones (ETDZs) are another type of industrial park focused on developing new industries and modern manufacturing. They are responsible for a significant portion of China's high-tech industrial output and exports.

The Future: Moving Up the Value Chain

Looking ahead, China's SEZs and industrial clusters face the challenge of moving up the global value chain. The focus is shifting towards more knowledge- and technology-based development, emphasizing domestic markets and consumption as sources of growth, and upgrading through technology innovation and learning.

Trade Routes and Major Ports

Navigating the Global Trade Winds

China's trade routes are the modern-day Silk Roads, carrying goods to and from every corner of the globe. These routes are not just about cargo; they are about connectivity, cooperation, and the exchange of cultures and ideas.

Major Ports: The Hubs of Commerce

China's coastline is dotted with ports, each a hub of activity and a gateway to the world. Here are some of the major ports that play a crucial role in international trade:

Shanghai Port: The world's busiest port, Shanghai is a deep-sea and riverine port that has established container cargo trade with over 500 ports in more than 200 countries.

Ningbo-Zhoushan Port: Located in Zhejiang province, this port has been the largest globally in terms of cargo throughput for several years, serving as a crucial hub for international trade.

Xiamen Port: An essential node of the 21st Century Maritime Silk Road, Xiamen Port has opened numerous container liner routes, including international, and internal branch lines, and domestic trade routes.

Guangzhou Port: The largest comprehensive main hub port in South China, Guangzhou Port has over 131 international container liner routes, connecting to more than 300 ports in over 100 countries.

Shenzhen Port: One of the most evolving ports in the region, Shenzhen serves as a feeder port and services nearly 10,000 vessels annually.

The Belt and Road Initiative: A New Era of Trade

The Belt and Road Initiative (BRI) has supercharged China's overseas port investment and construction activities. It aims to enhance regional connectivity and embrace the cultural and economic ties that once flourished along the ancient Silk Road.

China's Overseas Port Investments

China's maritime influence extends through investments in strategic overseas ports. The country operates or has ownership stakes in ports across every continent, reflecting its significant geoeconomic influence over international sea lanes and commercial ports.

The Future of Trade

Looking ahead, China's trade routes and ports are set to expand further. The country has signed numerous bilateral and regional shipping agreements, covering major countries and regions worldwide. China's shipping routes and service networks now encompass the globe, marking the nation as a leading commercial power.

Innovation and Technology Centers

The Cradle of Creativity: Innovation Hubs

China's innovation hubs are the cradle of creativity and technological advancement. These centers are not just about developing new products; they are about fostering an ecosystem where ideas can flourish and businesses can grow.

Beijing: The Capital of Innovation

Beijing, the capital city, is at the forefront of China's innovation drive. It is home to Zhongguancun, often dubbed "China's Silicon Valley," which hosts a high concentration of tech firms and startups. The city's emphasis on research and development has made it a leading destination for innovation in fields like artificial intelligence, biotechnology, and renewable energy.

Shanghai: The City of Tech Giants

Shanghai is another powerhouse of innovation, with its Pudong district being a magnet for tech giants and financial institutions. The city's blend of business acumen and technological expertise has given rise to cutting-edge developments in fintech, smart manufacturing, and digital services.

Shenzhen: The Hardware Silicon Valley

Shenzhen, once a small fishing village, has transformed into a global hub for electronics manufacturing and innovation. The city's unique ecosystem of hardware startups, OEM manufacturers, and design houses has made it a hotbed for technological breakthroughs, particularly in telecommunications and consumer electronics.

Guangdong-Hong Kong-Macao Greater Bay Area: A New Frontier

The Guangdong-Hong Kong-Macao Greater Bay Area is an ambitious project to create a world-class city cluster through the integration of innovation and technology. This region aims to become a global leader in advanced industries like robotics, clean energy, and next-generation information technology.

The Role of Government and Policy

The Chinese government plays a pivotal role in nurturing these innovation centers. Through policies, funding, and infrastructure support, it has created an environment conducive to technological advancement and entrepreneurship.

The Future: A Hub of Global Innovation

China's innovation centers are not just national treasures; they are becoming hubs of global innovation. With the government's support, these centers are attracting talent from around the world and establishing international partnerships to drive global technological progress.

CHAPTER 8

Natural Wonders and National Parks

China's Diverse Ecosystems and Conservation Areas

where we journey through China's breathtaking natural wonders and delve into the nation's efforts to conserve its rich biodiversity.

A Tapestry of Life: China's Ecosystems

China's vast land encompasses an array of ecosystems, each a tapestry of life, from the high-altitude plateaus of Tibet to the dense rainforests of Yunnan. The country's diverse landscapes harbor a wealth of flora and fauna, some of which are found nowhere else on Earth.

Forests: China's forests range from the cold-temperate coniferous forests of the north to the subtropical evergreen forests in the south. These green canopies are home to an array of wildlife, including the iconic giant panda and the elusive Amur leopard.

Grasslands: The rolling grasslands of Inner Mongolia and the Tibetan Plateau are grazing grounds for species like the Tibetan antelope and the Mongolian horse.

Wetlands: China's wetlands, such as the Poyang Lake and the Yellow River Delta, are vital stopovers for migratory birds and support rich aquatic biodiversity.

Deserts: The Gobi and Taklamakan deserts offer stark beauty and are ecosystems with unique species adapted to the harsh conditions.

Marine Areas: China's long coastline and marine areas are teeming with life, including coral reefs, mangroves, and a variety of marine species.

Conservation Efforts: Safeguarding Nature's Bounty

China has made significant strides in conservation, recognizing the importance of protecting its natural heritage.

Protected Areas: China has established a comprehensive network of protected areas, including nature reserves, national parks, and scenic areas, to safeguard its biodiversity.

National Parks: The country is setting up national parks, such as the Giant Panda National Park, to provide a sanctuary for endangered species and preserve ecological integrity.

Biodiversity Action Plans: China has implemented national strategies and action plans to address threats to biodiversity and promote sustainable use of natural resources.

International Cooperation: China actively participates in international conservation efforts and has ratified agreements like the Convention on Biological Diversity.

Challenges and Opportunities

Despite these efforts, China faces challenges in biodiversity conservation, such as habitat loss, pollution, and climate change. However, there are also opportunities to enhance conservation through scientific research, community involvement, and eco-tourism.

Famous Natural Attractions and Their Locations

Zhangjiajie's "Floating" Peaks

Location: Zhangjiajie National Forest Park, Hunan Province

Description: Known for its towering sandstone pillars, Zhangjiajie's landscape inspired the floating mountains in the movie "Avatar." The park is a UNESCO World Heritage site and offers breathtaking views, especially when the peaks are shrouded in mist.

Li River Karst Scenery

Location: Stretching from Guilin to Yangshuo, Guangxi Province

Description: The Li River is famed for its karst mountain scenery. A cruise along the river offers a serene experience with picturesque views of limestone peaks, rice paddies, and traditional villages.

Mount Everest

Location: Border of Tibet Autonomous Region and Nepal

Description: Mount Everest, the world's highest peak, provides awe-inspiring views and is a popular destination for trekkers looking to visit the base camp on the Tibetan side.

Tiger Leaping Gorge

Location: Yunnan Province

Description: One of the deepest and most spectacular river canyons in the world, Tiger Leaping Gorge offers hikers dramatic views of the Jinsha River and the surrounding mountains.

Jiuzhaigou Valley

Location: Sichuan Province

Description: Jiuzhaigou is a nature reserve known for its multi-level waterfalls, colorful lakes, and snow-capped peaks. It's a UNESCO World Heritage site and a habitat for the giant panda.

Yarlung Tsangpo Canyon

Location: Tibet Autonomous Region

Description: Often considered the deepest canyon in the world, Yarlung Tsangpo Canyon is a breathtakingly beautiful and remote area, offering some of the most challenging whitewater rafting in the world.

The Qiantang Tidal Bore

Location: Qiantang River, Zhejiang Province

Description: The Qiantang Tidal Bore is a natural phenomenon where the leading edge of the incoming tide forms waves that travel up a river against the direction of the river's current. It's one of the largest tidal bores in the world.

Zhangye Danxia Landform

Location: Gansu Province

Description: The Zhangye Danxia landform area is known for its colorful rock formations, often referred to as the "Rainbow Mountains." The unique geological structure creates a stunning, layered appearance.

Ecotourism and Environmental Protection

Ecotourism in China is an approach to tourism that respects and celebrates the country's natural heritage while promoting conservation and sustainable travel. It's about creating an immersive experience that allows visitors to connect with nature and learn about the local environment and culture.

Principles of Ecotourism: The core of ecotourism is to minimize the impact on the environment, support the protection of natural areas, and empower local communities. It encourages responsible travel to natural areas that conserves the environment and improves the well-being of local people.

Popular Ecotourism Destinations: China offers a plethora of ecotourism destinations, from the panda sanctuaries in Sichuan to the tropical paradise of Hainan. Each destination provides a unique opportunity to witness China's biodiversity and efforts in environmental conservation.

Environmental Protection: A National Priority

China's commitment to environmental protection is evident in its policies and actions. The country has made significant progress in addressing environmental challenges, such as air and water pollution, and is actively working towards a more sustainable future.

Conservation Measures: China has implemented a range of conservation measures, including establishing protected areas, promoting afforestation programs, and investing in renewable energy sources.

Challenges and Solutions: Despite these efforts, challenges remain, such as balancing economic growth with environmental sustainability. China continues to explore innovative solutions, such as green technology and eco-friendly urban planning, to overcome these challenges.

The Role of Ecotourism in Conservation

Ecotourism plays a vital role in China's environmental protection efforts by:

Raising Awareness: Ecotourism helps raise public awareness about the importance of nature conservation and the need for sustainable living practices.

Supporting Local Economies: By directing tourism revenue to local communities, ecotourism supports sustainable economic development and incentivizes conservation efforts.

Promoting Cultural Exchange: Ecotourism fosters a greater understanding and appreciation of China's diverse cultures and traditions, which are often closely tied to the natural environment.

Looking Ahead: Sustainable Tourism

As China continues to develop its ecotourism sector, the focus is on ensuring that it remains sustainable and beneficial for both the environment and the people. This includes:

Regulating Ecotourism Activities: Implementing strict guidelines and regulations to ensure that ecotourism activities do not harm the environment.

Encouraging Responsible Travel: Promoting responsible travel practices among tourists, such as following leave-no-trace principles and supporting eco-friendly businesses.

Investing in Research and Development: Investing in research to better understand the impacts of tourism on the environment and to develop new ways to mitigate these impacts.

Traveler's Guide to Dining, Shopping, and Accommodation.

Culinary Delights: Best Places to Eat

China's culinary landscape is as vast and varied as the country itself. Here are some top cities renowned for their food:

Hong Kong: A culinary powerhouse, offering everything from Cantonese cuisine and dim sum to international dishes.

Beijing: Famous for Peking duck and a variety of wheat foods like noodles and dumplings.

Chengdu: The heart of Sichuan cuisine, perfect for those who love spicy food with dishes like Kung Pao chicken and mapo tofu.

Average Price Range: Dining in China can range from a few dollars for street food to over $100 for a luxurious meal at a high-end restaurant.

Retail Therapy: Shopping Destinations

China is a shopper's paradise, with bustling markets and modern malls. Some famous shopping streets include:

Wangfujing Street, Beijing: Offers a mix of large department stores, souvenir shops, and food stalls.

Chunxi Road, Chengdu: Home to brand stores, boutiques, and local snacks.

Shangxiajiu Pedestrian Street, Guangzhou: Features unique architecture and a variety of shops.

Average Price Range: Shopping in China can vary greatly, from a few dollars for souvenirs to thousands for luxury goods.

Restful Retreats: Accommodation Options

Accommodations in China cater to all preferences and budgets, from luxury hotels to budget hostels.

Luxury Hotels: Expect to pay around $100-200+ per night for five-star accommodations.

Mid-range Hotels: Prices range from $20-60+ per night for a comfortable stay.

Budget Hotels: For budget-conscious travelers, accommodations can be as low as $3-15 per night.

Booking Tips:

Book in Advance: Especially during peak seasons to secure better rates.

Compare Prices: Use online platforms to find the best deals.

Consider Location: Staying a bit further from tourist hotspots can reduce costs.

Read Reviews: Look for recent reviews to gauge quality and service.

CHAPTER 9

Cultural Tapestry

Ethnolinguistic Groups and Distribution

A Mosaic of Peoples

China is a mosaic of different peoples, each with their languages, traditions, and histories. The Han Chinese form the majority, but there are 55 officially recognized ethnic minority groups, making up about 8.49% of the population.

The Zhuang: The largest minority, primarily found in the Guangxi Zhuang Autonomous Region.

The Uyghurs: Concentrated in Xinjiang Uyghur Autonomous Region, known for their rich cultural heritage.

The Hui: Widespread throughout China, with significant populations in the Ningxia Hui Autonomous Region.

The Miao: Residing mainly in Guizhou and Hunan provinces, famous for their vibrant festivals and intricate silver jewelry.

The Tibetans: Living on the "roof of the world" in Tibet Autonomous Region, guardians of a unique Buddhist culture.

Language Families

The languages spoken by China's ethnic groups belong to several major language families:

Sino-Tibetan: Encompassing Mandarin and the languages of many other ethnic groups like the Yi and the Bai.

Altaic: Including the Turkic languages of the Uyghurs and the Mongolic languages of the Mongols.

Indo-European: Represented by the Tajik and Russian ethnic groups.

Austroasiatic: Spoken by some of the smaller groups in southern China, such as the Wa and the De'ang.

Cultural Preservation and Promotion

China's government has policies in place to preserve and promote the cultures of its ethnic minorities. This includes support for cultural festivals, traditional arts, and the use of minority languages in education and media.

Distribution and Demographics

The distribution of ethnolinguistic groups is diverse:

> ➢ Northwest and North: Home to the Uyghurs, Hui, and Mongols.
> ➢ Northeast: The Manchus and Koreans.
> ➢ Southwest: A multitude of groups, including the Tibetans, Miao, and Yi.
> ➢ South: The Zhuang and other Tai-speaking peoples.

Challenges and Opportunities

While China celebrates its cultural diversity, there are challenges, such as ensuring equitable development and addressing regional disparities. However, there are also opportunities for cultural exchange and the enrichment of the national identity through diversity.

Cultural Festivals and Traditions

A Calendar of Celebrations

China's festivals are a colorful tapestry that weaves together the threads of history, tradition, and community. Here are some of the most significant festivals celebrated across the nation:

Chinese New Year (Spring Festival): Marking the beginning of the lunar new year, this is China's most important festival. Families gather for reunion dinners, homes are decorated with red lanterns, and the air is filled with the crackle of firecrackers.

Lantern Festival: Celebrated on the 15th day of the first lunar month, it marks the end of Chinese New Year festivities. Lanterns light up the night, and people enjoy sweet rice balls called tangyuan.

Qingming Festival (Tomb Sweeping Day): A time for honoring ancestors, families visit graves to pay their respects. It's also a time to enjoy the beauty of spring.

Dragon Boat Festival: Commemorating the poet Qu Yuan, dragon boat races are held, and zongzi (sticky rice dumplings) are eaten.

Mid-Autumn Festival: Also known as the Mooncake Festival, it's a time for family reunions and moon gazing.

Mooncakes, a rich pastry filled with sweet or savory fillings, are a traditional treat.

Traditions That Bind

Each festival is steeped in tradition, with customs that have been passed down through generations:

Red Envelopes: During Chinese New Year, red envelopes filled with money are given to children and unmarried adults for good luck.

Lion and Dragon Dances: These dances are performed during various festivals to bring prosperity and ward off evil spirits.

Kite Flying: A popular activity during Qingming Festival, it symbolizes the sending of blessings to the heavens.

Wearing New Clothes: It's customary to wear new clothes during festivals, signifying a fresh start and the welcoming of good fortune.

The Essence of Chinese Culture

Festivals and traditions are the essence of Chinese culture. They are a reflection of the values, beliefs, and collective memory of the people. Through the celebration of these festivals, the rich tapestry of China's history is honored and preserved.

Embracing the Future

While deeply rooted in the past, China's cultural festivals and traditions are evolving. Modern elements are being incorporated, and the festivals are becoming platforms for cultural exchange and global participation.

Culinary Diversity Across Regions

Northern Delights: Wheat and Warmth

In the north, the cuisine is hearty and robust, reflecting the colder climate. Wheat-based dishes like noodles, dumplings, and steamed buns are staples. Beijing's Peking Duck, with its crispy skin and succulent meat, is a must-try, as are the Mongolian hotpot and Inner Mongolian roasted whole lamb.

Eastern Elegance: Subtle and Sweet

Eastern China's cuisine is known for its delicate flavors and emphasis on freshness. Seafood plays a significant role, with dishes like Shanghai's sweet and sour fish and Zhejiang's Dongpo pork, a slow-cooked, melt-in-your-mouth experience.

Spicy Central: Heat and Harmony

Central China, particularly Sichuan and Hunan provinces, is famous for its spicy food. The use of Sichuan peppercorns adds a unique numbing sensation to dishes like mapo tofu and kung pao chicken.

Southern Savors: Diversity and Dim Sum

The south is renowned for its diversity, with Guangdong (Cantonese) cuisine leading the way. Dim sum, a variety of small, bite-sized dishes served in bamboo steamers, is a highlight. The sour flavors of minority cuisines in regions like Yunnan and Guizhou add a tangy twist to the southern palate.

Western Wholesomeness: Halal and Hearty

Western China's cuisine reflects its Muslim heritage, with halal food featuring prominently. Lamb is the meat of choice, often seasoned with cumin and other spices, and served in dishes like hand-pulled noodles and grilled skewers.

Fusion and Future: The Evolving Table

China's culinary scene is not static; it's a fusion of tradition and innovation. New flavors and techniques are constantly being incorporated, creating an ever-evolving table that reflects the dynamic nature of Chinese society.

CONCLUSION

Charting the Course of China's Journey

As we draw the "China Atlas Road Map 2024" to a close, we reflect on the journey we've embarked upon—a journey through time, space, and the collective narrative of a nation that stands as a testament to human endeavor and ambition.

Reflections on China's Past, Present, and Future

China's story is one of profound transformation. From the ancient dynasties that laid the foundations of civilization to the modern powerhouse reshaping the global order, China's past is a tapestry woven with threads of innovation, resilience, and cultural richness. Today, China stands at a crossroads, balancing its rich heritage with the aspirations of a future where it seeks to play a leading role on the world stage. The road map for 2024 and beyond is not just a set of directions; it is a vision of progress, sustainability, and harmony—a vision that China is determined to realize.

The Role of the Atlas in Education and Policy-Making

This atlas serves as more than a collection of maps and narratives; it is an educational tool that enlightens minds and informs policy-making. It provides a window into the complexities of China's geography, demography, and socio-economic fabric, offering insights that are crucial for scholars, students, and decision-makers alike. By charting the contours of China's landscapes, both natural and human-made, the atlas equips us with the knowledge to understand the forces that shape China's policies and its interactions with the world.

Final Thoughts on China's Road Map for 2024 and Beyond

As we contemplate China's road map for 2024 and beyond, we are reminded that the journey of a nation is never a solitary one. It is a path shared with the global community, marked by mutual challenges and shared destinies. China's future, as outlined in this atlas, is not merely a projection of its ambitions but a blueprint for engagement, cooperation, and mutual growth.

The "China Atlas Road Map 2024" is a guide, a companion, and a chronicle of a nation's quest for advancement while staying true to its roots. It is a reminder that while the landscapes may change, the essence of a nation—its people, its culture, and its dreams—remains constant.

As we close this chapter and look to the horizon, let us carry with us the understanding that maps do more than chart territories—they chart possibilities, potentials, and the promise of a shared future. May the "China Atlas Road Map 2024" inspire you to explore, learn, and appreciate the intricate mosaic that is China.

Journey Onward

With the conclusion of this atlas, we invite you to continue the journey, explore the world beyond its pages, and see for yourself the landscapes, the people, and the spirit of China. The road ahead is long, but it is paved with the aspirations of a nation that is both ancient and youthful, traditional and innovative, local and global. Let us step forward with curiosity, respect, and an open mind, ready to embrace the road that lies ahead

Made in United States
Troutdale, OR
07/08/2024

21095571R00066